American
GROUND FORCES
in the Vietnam War

HUNTER KEETER

WORLD ALMANAC® LIBRARY

Please visit our web site at: www.worldalmanaclibrary.com
For a free color catalog describing World Almanac® Library's list of high-quality books
and multimedia programs, call 1-800-848-2928 (USA) or 1-800-387-3178 (Canada).
World Almanac® Library's fax: (414) 332-3567.

Library of Congress Cataloging-in-Publication Data

Keeter, Hunter.
    American ground forces in the Vietnam War / by Hunter Keeter.
      p. cm. — (The American experience in Vietnam)
    Includes bibliographical references and index.
    ISBN 0-8368-5774-7 (lib. bdg.)
    ISBN 0-8368-5781-X (softcover)
    1. Vietnamese Conflict, 1961-1975—United States—Juvenile literature. 2. United States Army—
History—Vietnamese Conflict, 1961-1975—Juvenile literature. 3. United States Marine Corps—
History—Vietnamese Conflict, 1961-1975—Juvenile literature. I. Title. II. Series.
    DS558.K44   2005
    959.704'342—dc22   2004058090

First published in 2005 by
World Almanac® Library
330 West Olive Street, Suite 100
Milwaukee, WI 53212 USA

Copyright © 2005 by World Almanac® Library.

Developed by Amber Books Ltd.
Editor: James Bennett
Designer: Colin Hawes
Photo research: Natasha Jones
World Almanac® Library editors: Mark Sachner and Alan Wachtel
World Almanac® Library art direction: Tammy West
World Almanac® Library production: Jessica Morris

Picture Acknowledgements
Camera Press: 36; Cody Images (www.codyimages.com): cover (top left), 1, 4 (top left), 11, 16,
18, 19, 20, 22, 24, 25, 33, 35; Corbis: cover (main), 6, 7, 8, 10, 12, 14, 15, 21, 26, 28, 29, 30,
32, 34, 38, 40, 42, 43; Getty Images: 39.

Printed in Canada

1 2 3 4 5 6 7 8 9 09 08 07 06 05

About the Author

HUNTER KEETER is a journalist with *Defense Daily*, a leading defense
business publication. He is the author of the *Homeland Security* and *U.S.
Marines* volumes in the *America's Armed Forces* series from World Almanac®
Library. Before becoming a writer he earned an MA in Literature and
Education and worked as a schoolteacher. He lives in Arlington, Virginia.

Table of Contents

Words that appear in the glossary are printed in **boldface** type the first time they occur in the text

Introduction

The Vietnam War (1954–1975) was part of a larger conflict known as the Second Indochina War, which raged in Southeast Asia and involved the nations of Cambodia, Laos, and Vietnam. From 1946 until 1954, the Vietnamese had fought for independence from France during the First Indochina War. When the French were defeated, the country was divided into North and South Vietnam. Vietnamese communists controlled North Vietnam and wanted to unify Vietnam under communist rule. Non-communist Vietnamese controlled the South. In the 1950s, the United States and the Soviet Union were in the early years of their struggle over political, economic, and military influence in various parts of the world. Known as the Cold War, this struggle did not pit each nation against the other directly. Rather, each supported other countries that were squared off against one another. In the 1950s, the United States began training South Vietnam's army, while the Soviet Union and China backed communist North Vietnam. By the mid-1960s, U.S. forces fought alongside the Army of the Republic of Vietnam (ARVN) against the North Vietnamese Army (NVA) and the National Front for the Liberation of Vietnam (NLF).

One of the most challenging aspects for the ground forces who fought in Vietnam was the fact that it could at times be impossible to tell North Vietnamese troops, many of whom did not wear proper uniforms, from South Vietnamese civilians. The terrain, too, presented a challenge for the military. The war was fought in villages and rice paddies, in thick swampy jungles, and in twisting river ways.

Some recruits had been drafted into service; others volunteered. Regardless of how they got there, arrival at boot camp provided an abrupt introduction to what lay ahead. At boot camp, recruits received combat training and were **indoctrinated** into military society and culture. After boot camp was over and the recruits had been turned into soldiers, it was off to Vietnam and life in the field. New arrivals were often surprised to learn that the Vietnam War was being fought on two fronts. One was a fairly conventional war against the NVA. The other was a **guerrilla** war against the Viet Cong.

Soldiers in Vietnam coped with the stresses and horrors of war in a number of different ways. Some spent their free time cleaning their equipment and weapons to be ready for the next patrol. Others engaged in games such as baseball and volleyball and had barbecues to try to remind themselves of home. For soldiers on leave, drug use and use of prostitutes were major problems, and the U.S. military had to adopt policies to combat these growing threats.

As the war dragged on and more and more soldiers were killed, protests and demonstrations against the U.S. presence in Vietnam grew. Members of the counterculture movement of the 1960s questioned authority and championed self-expression. The war represented everything they loathed and stirred up strong, passionate protests in the United States. Soldiers returning from Vietnam often found themselves the targets of scorn and ridicule. In 1982, the Vietnam Veterans Memorial was dedicated in Washington, D.C., to commemorate the personnel who died or were declared missing in action in Vietnam.

Below: This map shows North and South Vietnam and the surrounding area. Key regions, cities, and military bases are indicated.

5

CHAPTER 1: Basic Training

Boot Camp

Right: At boot camp, recruits were challenged on courses that included obstacles such as this barbed wire at Fort Dix, New Jersey. The goal was for recruits to learn the skills and determination to overcome the challenges they would face while on active duty.

Young men in the United States who enlisted, or who were compelled to join the armed forces in a system known as the draft, first reported to a military entrance processing center. At the center, medical personnel decided if a potential recruit was fit for duty. A recruit had to strip off his street clothes and stand barefoot on a tile floor in long lines with other recruits, waiting to be seen by a physician. The physician examined a recruit for problems or diseases, such as flat-footedness or tuberculosis, that could disqualify him from military service. When a recruit was found medically fit for duty, he went on to basic training, known as boot camp. Each of the U.S. military services—the Air Force, Army, Coast Guard, Navy, and Marine Corps—had separate boot camps. Basic training facilities were located in several places in the United States. The army managed a large infantry training center at Fort Dix, New Jersey. The Marine Corps Recruit Training Depot, Parris Island, located near Beaufort, South Carolina, was the first stop for many recruits on their way to the war.

THE BASICS OF BOOT CAMP

During the eight to twelve weeks of boot camp, drill instructors—usually older and more experienced non-commissioned officers—indoctrinated civilians into military culture and provided them with a basic knowledge of military skills. Each of the services placed different emphases on military skills; for example, a marine recruit

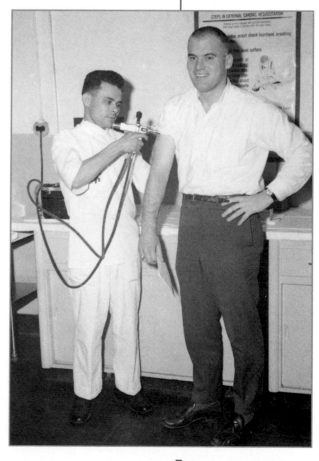

Below: All new recruits—even former professional football players like Pete Gogolak of the New York Giants, pictured here—had to pass a physical examination and be inoculated against common diseases.

THE DRAFT

Beginning in 1940, to increase the size of its armed forces in time of war or national emergency, the United States government administered the Selective Service System, backed by a law called the Military Selective Service Act, to compel young men to serve in the military. In the early years of the Vietnam War, local draft boards were free to call up whomever they chose, selecting men at random from lists held for their districts. From 1969, the Selective Service System operated as a national lottery, also known as the draft. The law required men between the ages of eighteen and twenty-five to register and be assigned a lottery number. When the government selected a person's lottery number, he was required to report for military service. Young men could avoid being drafted by voluntarily enlisting; volunteers could choose the military branch in which they served. Men could defer their draft number by enrolling in a university or by demonstrating they were unfit for military service. Today, eighteen-year-old men who are U.S. citizens are still required to register with the Selective Service System. Since 1973, however, there has been no draft, and each of the U.S. military services takes pride in being an all-volunteer force.

Above: Until 1973, the Selective Service System managed the draft, which compelled young men above the age of eighteen to enter military service. The draftees' numbers were drawn from rotating cylinders and matched to the Selective Service registration list.

received more intensive **infantry** combat training than an air force airman recruit.

Army recruits were schooled for eight weeks in basic combat training and then received eight weeks of advanced individual training, where they learned the skills associated with their military occupational specialty (MOS). A soldier's MOS was his job. An army MOS was assigned a number and letter code, such as "11-Bravo" for infantry or "13-Alpha" for field **artillery**. The marines used a different system. The designation for basic infantry was "0300," and the designation for basic field artillery was "0800."

MARINE BOOT CAMP

Different military branches had different types of boot camp. The Marine Corps boot camp is being used here as an example of how they were run. Recruits between the ages of seventeen and twenty-eight were enlisted for periods of two, four, or six years. Marine Corps boot camp lasted twelve weeks, including an intense indoctrination into the culture of the Marine Corps. Physical fitness challenges, marksmanship training, basic field skills, such as survival and orienteering, and close-order drill, such as marching and handling a rifle, were all taught. A recruit marine stepped off the bus at the training depot and stood at attention on painted yellow footprints beside other recruits while a drill instructor sternly stated they "had been removed from all the creature comforts of civilian society and [were] in a military environment." For many, that was to change their lives forever.

Early on, recruit marines had to endure head shaving, stripping away the appearance of individuality to emphasize membership in the Corps. Head shaving also had practical benefits. It stopped lice from spreading and made head wounds easier to treat. Recruits also put away their civilian clothes. The training depot issued each

Right: As the counterculture movement gained momentum, and public dissatisfaction with the Vietnam War intensified, many protested the Selective Service System by burning their draft cards and ignoring the government's call to service.

1960s CULTURE AND THE DRAFT

The draft became controversial in the 1960s and 1970s, as many citizens opposed the United States' involvement in Southeast Asia. Even senior U.S. government officials doubted the war. For example, Robert S. McNamara, the U.S. Secretary of Defense from 1965 to 1968, knew the war he had planned and managed could not be won and believed the United States should have withdrawn from Vietnam. During the war, however, McNamara did not publicly share his views. Hundreds of thousands of U.S. citizens protested against the war in rallies and marches. Some protested against the Selective Service System by burning their numbered draft cards. Some escaped the draft by leaving the United States, often moving to Canada. The derogatory term "draft dodger" was used to describe men who avoided the Selective Service System.

new man a green cotton battle-dress uniform, black leather combat boots, and a cap. Instructors kept up the physical and mental pressure on recruits every day, from the **reveille** bugle call at 5:00 A.M. until lights-out in the **squad** bays at 9:00 P.M. According to Sergeant Major Alfonso Villa, the Marine Corps boot camp experience was unpleasant but sometimes comical. "I'm in boot camp, and I'm miserable. I'm thinking, 'I could've gone to jail and been better off.'" He said, "[The] drill instructors

Below: These recruits at Fort Polk, Louisiana, are being taught to fight in a mock tunnel system similar to that used by Viet Cong guerrillas.

Above: U.S. Marine Corps drill instructors were renowned for their toughness with new recruits, keeping up the pressure, mentally and physically, and testing each man to his breaking point.

yelled and screamed [and] called us names we had never even dreamed of. I was always getting in trouble because I would laugh." Getting into trouble during boot camp usually led to punishment in the form of intense physical exercise, such as "dropping" for push-ups and "falling-in" for long runs.

Drill instructors demanded recruits learn how to wear their uniforms properly, how to salute, and how to address superiors. Every marine drill instructor told his recruits, "The first word and the last word out of your mouth will be 'Sir'!" A drill instructor also showed recruits how to maintain and shoot a weapon—usually an M14 rifle—and basic hand-to-hand combat techniques. Each recruit had to pass thirty-three hours of academic instruction. These

VIETNAM-ERA MILITARY SLANG

An **AO** was an area of operations.

A **bird** was any aircraft, especially helicopters.

The **boonies** and the **bush** were terms for remote jungles, forests, and swamps.

U.S. troops had many names for their NVA and Viet Cong enemies. Some of these terms came from the military phonetic pronunciation of the letters **VC**, such as **Victor Charlie**, or **Charlie**.

U.S. troops often had to get **clearance**, or permission, before attacking, unless they were fired upon.

Didi mau was derived from the Vietnamese words for "leave quickly."

Dinky dau meant crazy.

Dung lai meant stop.

A **firefight** was a gun battle.

Gung ho, derived from Chinese or Korean, meant highly motivated.

A **Hot LZ** was a helicopter landing zone under attack.

Humping meant marching, usually carrying a heavy backpack.

Khong xau meant no problem.

KIA meant killed in action, and **MIA** meant missing in action.

In Country meant being in Vietnam.

Light up and **rock and roll** meant to open fire.

Number One meant something was best; **Number Ten** meant something was worst.

Soldiers **saddled up**—took up their TA-50, which meant field equipment, such as boots, ponchos, web gear, and canteens—before going out on patrol.

Tracks were armored personnel carriers and tanks.

Walking point meant being the first man in line on patrol.

Wasted or **zapped** meant killed.

The **world** was home, the United States.

Xin loi meant sorry.

Below: An army drill sergeant shows recruits a bayonet drill. Teaching even apparently obsolete hand-to-hand combat techniques was an important part of recruit training to help build aggression and confidence.

lessons taught recruits to value and develop the qualities—such as courage and loyalty—by which they were expected to live during their enlistment. Recruit marines also learned the Marine Corps' motto, *Semper Fidelis*, Latin for "Always Faithful."

Sergeant Major Villa remembered his drill instructor issuing one final warning on the night before his graduation. The drill instructor separated the **platoon** into thirds and said to one group, "You guys are going to Vietnam and not coming back." To a second group the drill instructor said, "You guys are going to have auto accidents ... and will never make it through your first tour." To the third group he said, "You guys will probably make the Marine Corps a career."

SOUTHEAST ASIA: CLIMATE AND TERRAIN

The landscape and climate of Southeast Asia is remarkably different from that of most of the United States. For example, Highway One was then, and is today, the only paved road running the length of Vietnam. Recruits not only had to develop military skills, but also had to learn to survive in an alien, challenging environment. To prepare them for the reality of fighting in tropical, thickly forested, mountainous Southeast Asia, simulations of Vietnam's terrain were developed for the training of recruits.

For much of the year, Vietnam is tropically warm and humid, with heavy rainfall during the monsoon season between May and October. The average temperature in Hanoi is 74° Fahrenheit (23° Celsius), while Saigon averages 78° F (26° C). The climate is damp, especially in the south, averaging 80 percent humidity. Each year has about one hundred days of rainfall. Many rivers cut through Vietnam, from Cambodia and Laos down to the deltas and the Gulf of Tonkin. The most prominent man-made features are rice paddies, with bicycle tracks and footpaths running along the tops of them.

Above: A patrol of U.S. soldiers make their way along a rice paddy field in the Tan An Delta.

15

"In Country"

Right: An infantryman stands watch amid the elephant grass with his M16 automatic rifle. Soldiers had to be vigilant as Viet Cong guerrillas often ambushed U.S. patrols and then vanished quickly into the dense foliage.

The Vietnam War differed from other conflicts U.S. military forces had faced during the twentieth century, in that U.S. troops were simultaneously fighting two distinct wars. On the one hand, they fought a more or less conventional war against the NVA, a well-organized, uniformed military force, backed by money and equipment from the Soviet Union and China. The NVA fought using regular infantry, artillery, tanks, and aircraft. On the other hand, U.S. troops faced a guerrilla war against the Viet Cong. A guerrilla force avoids open battle with its larger and stronger enemy, but instead stealthily harasses, demoralizes, and weakens its enemy by striking many small blows and evading capture.

THE VIET CONG

The Viet Cong were dangerous. They could disguise themselves as civilians and hide in the villages through which soldiers patrolled. Sometimes, the Viet Cong created hidden fortresses in the backcountry, forcing civilian villagers to support the Viet Cong troops' activities and to give them shelter, food, and supplies. The Viet Cong also demanded information about U.S. forces. One captured Viet Cong told U.S. and South Vietnamese government authorities, "Children were trained to throw grenades, not only for the terror factor, but so the government or American soldiers would have to shoot them. Then the Americans feel very ashamed and they blame themselves and call their soldiers war criminals."

One U.S. officer summed up the hard task of confronting the Viet Cong:

"The most difficult part of the battle was deciding when we were going to win … and what price we were going to pay to do it. We had to think and remind ourselves that we could eliminate the Viet Cong but might also eliminate … civilians who were not Viet Cong, who were just afraid, who were being held hostage, or who were trying to hide and became victims of the war."

Right: While "search-and-destroy" became a characteristic phrase for combat missions in Vietnam, often U.S. soldiers sought to capture Viet Cong guerrillas, as shown here. Intelligence officers interrogated prisoners to learn more about how the VC worked.

LESSONS TO LEARN

The first combat veterans in Vietnam had not yet had a chance to teach the lessons they had learned. Consequently, many new marines and soldiers arrived in Vietnam unprepared, sometimes being wounded or killed before they even had a chance to learn. Lieutenant General Jefferson D. Howell, Jr., commander of Marine Forces Pacific, said, "We learned a lot of lessons in blood … because of our lack of training."

Another Lieutenant General described an average soldier:

"[He was] a boy, about 19 years of age, armed and in uniform, who did not choose to be [in Vietnam]. He would have preferred to remain at home, comfortable, enjoying the many attractions and conveniences available to Americans; secure in the company of his family, his friends, his sweetheart."

As had his peers in other wars, the soldier in Vietnam confronted fear. Perhaps more clearly than at any other period of U.S. history to date, vivid images of battle goaded the fear of a

BOOBY TRAPS

The VC were expert at preparing booby traps for unwary or careless U.S. troops. Guerrillas forced rural villagers to make these deadly devices. Some booby traps were technically simple, such as punji stake pits. Civilian women and children were made to dig a shallow pit, into the bottom of which sharp bamboo or metal stakes were driven. They covered the top of the pit with leaves and earth to make it appear like solid ground. When a "grunt" (the nickname for infantry soldiers) stepped on the cover, he crashed through onto the spikes in the pit.

Other traps used explosives, such as Chinese-made antipersonnel mines and hand grenades. Often, Viet Cong guerrillas stretched a trip wire from a hidden grenade's pin, just high enough to catch a passing soldier's boot. The boot snagging the wire would pull out the grenade's pin, and it would explode behind the grunt.

Another type of booby trap was called a Rat Trap. This device was a box fastened to a tree trunk or other solid base, pointing into the soldier's path. Inside the Rat Trap were three .30-caliber rifle cartridges loaded into three short barrels. Spring-loaded nails were cocked behind each cartridge. When a soldier's boot touched a trip wire, the nails snapped onto the cartridges' primers, firing the bullets.

Above: Backed by an M48 tank, a soldier with the 101st Airborne Division stands guard while an engineer locates a mine.

Right: The ability to land troops anywhere by helicopter proved immensely valuable to U.S. forces. These soldiers of the 173rd Airborne Division are pictured leaping from a helicopter in a landing zone in June 1965.

BATTLE FOR THE IA DRANG VALLEY

The first all-out battle between U.S. and North Vietnamese forces was a victory for the U.S. Army's First Battalion, Seventh **Cavalry**, First Cavalry Division (Airmobile).

The Ia Drang Valley was a tactically important area of South Vietnam's Central Highlands. In the autumn of 1965, the U.S. Army launched airmobile excursions—helicopter-borne infantry assaults—into the valley to probe for enemy activity. A large North Vietnamese infantry force under the command of General Chu Huy Man was in the valley. The general's aim was to drive into South Vietnam and seize several important provinces. After Man's forces attacked a U.S. Special Forces camp at Plei Me, members of the First Cavalry Division pursued them into the Ia Drang Valley. On November 14, 1965, U.S. Army Lieutenant Colonel Harold G. Moore, Jr., led his men on a fateful mission.

UH-1D Huey helicopters carried 450 cavalry troopers to landing zones inside the North Vietnamese-held area. Overhead, UH-1D helicopter gunships armed with rockets and machine guns provided fire support in case of trouble.

At a landing zone code-named X-Ray, the first wave of U.S. cavalry troopers dismounted from their helicopters, right into the waiting fire of their enemies. Hidden in the hills were three North Vietnamese regiments supported by heavy artillery.

The battle raged for two days, both sides exchanging intense fire from artillery, mortars, rockets, grenades, machine guns, and automatic rifles.

In one incident, Lieutenant Joe Marm, leader of the Second Platoon, Bravo Company, 1/7 Cavalry, earned the Congressional Medal of Honor for his heroism. Under heavy fire, Marm single-handedly attacked a North Vietnamese position with hand grenades and his M16 assault rifle. Later in the action, Marm was shot in the face but survived.

According to Moore, American casualties included 79 killed and 121 wounded. At least 634 North Vietnamese soldiers were killed. The success of the smaller U.S. force was due in large part to airmobile fighting tactics. U.S. helicopters were used to land troops behind enemy fighting lines, evacuate wounded, and bring in reinforcements and supplies. The North Vietnamese, though well-armed and trained, were not as flexible a force.

SPECIAL FORCES

In May 1961, President John F. Kennedy ordered the Defense Department to expand U.S. special operations forces. Special operations forces—who came from the senior enlisted ranks of the conventional military—were educated in the cultures, languages, and regions in which they operated. U.S. military authorities at first distrusted special operations forces because these troops were viewed as slightly renegade, operating outside the normal chains of command. Eventually, the conventional military and special operations forces developed close working relationships. U.S. Army Special Forces—also called "Green Berets"—were among the most famous, along with the navy's Sea, Air, Land (SEAL) commando teams and the air force's Air Commandos. Special operations forces often worked closely with native groups, such as the Hmong, Khmer Krom, Montagnard, and Nung tribes. These native groups were not friendly to the communists and effectively worked against the NVA, Viet Cong, and others.

Right: A U.S. Army Special Forces officer uses his compass to demonstrate orienteering skills to a group of South Vietnamese soldiers. Because of their extensive education and extremely rigorous training, Special Forces were well qualified to instruct friendly troops.

Vietnam War-era soldier long before he actually took part in combat. By the late 1960s, the war was being televised. Each night, it was common for American families to eat supper together and watch the evening news programs, which showed the public near real-time films of actual battles and their consequences—violence, wounding, and death.

A REASON TO FIGHT

While U.S. political and military leaders in Washington, D.C., often spoke of the war as a fight for freedom and democracy, soldiers often fought it for much more personal reasons. Marine Corps Sergeant Tom Matteo said, "I fought each day to stay alive and to help my friends stay alive. I did not engage in combat for any other reason. Your decisions save and take lives, and combat is a toss of the coin at times. You normally have the capability to control your destiny in civilian life, but combat controls you."

Sometimes the way soldiers rotated through their thirteen-month tours of duty worked against the group loyalty of which Matteo spoke. Often grunts were sent home just as they acquired enough experience to be effective against the NVA and the Viet Cong. The replacements did not have this experience, and a U.S. fighting unit's learning curve was reset.

Active duty was an intense and exhausting experience. Infantrymen spent more than one hundred hours each week on patrol or manning an outpost. Operations continued around the clock, every day. Grunts were constantly under tremendous

Above: Many infantrymen who served during the Vietnam War were young men, around nineteen years of age, who looked forward to going home and rejoining their peers in civilian society.

23

MY LAI

Right: In the United States, there was public outrage over the fate of Army First Lieutenant William L. Calley, Jr., the only man convicted of war crimes after the massacre at My Lai.

Some events from the war underscored the very worst sort of inhumanity. On March 16, 1968, army commanders sent Task Force Barker—three companies of infantry, backed by an artillery battery, nine transport helicopters, and gunships—on a search-and-destroy mission against the Viet Cong's Forty-eighth Battalion. The army had learned that the Viet Cong were operating at Son My Village, a place that included the hamlets Co Luy, My Khe, and My Lai. Lieutenant Colonel Frank Barker commanded the task force. Captain Ernest Medina commanded C Company, with First Lieutenant William L. Calley, Jr., leading its First Platoon. The leaders of the task force believed that more than two hundred Viet Cong guerrillas were in or near Son My Village. According to testimony by some of those present, the U.S. troops moved into the village and its hamlets expecting a fight.

With helicopters hovering overhead, the soldiers of C

Company searched for the Viet Cong and for weapons or other supplies possibly hidden in the village. A farmer standing in a rice paddy waved at one of the helicopters. Suddenly, the aircraft's M60 machine-gunner opened fire, killing the farmer. Although no Viet Cong had been seen and no one had shot at the soldiers, C Company's First, Second, and Third Platoons fired bursts from their M16 automatic rifles and launched 1.5-inch (40-mm) high-explosive grenades, setting fire to the huts. The mission descended into four hours of murderous chaos. Army Major Anthony Raimondo, a military lawyer, said Task Force Barker killed four hundred to five hundred civilians at My Lai. "To this day, [however], we do not have an exact figure because of the inadequate investigations," he added.

Army Chief Warrant Officer Hugh C. Thompson, Jr., was credited with stopping the massacre. He landed his scout helicopter at the village and ordered his crew to shoot U.S. soldiers if they did not cease firing on the civilians. Two other helicopters joined Thompson to evacuate some of the civilians. Although several soldiers and officers were tried for the atrocities at My Lai, Lieutenant Calley was the only soldier found guilty by a **court-martial.** On March 31, 1971, Calley was sentenced to life in prison with hard labor. On April 15, 1974, the army reduced his sentence to ten years. At the U.S. Disciplinary Barracks, Fort Leavenworth, Kansas, he served four months as a clerk. On November 9, 1974, Calley was **paroled**.

Above: Heavy-lift helicopters, such as this CH-47, brought ammunition and other supplies to men manning remote firebases. The soldiers of this artillery unit have set up howitzers and are preparing sandbagged bunkers to protect machine gun nests.

physical, mental, and emotional pressure, especially on patrol. Marine Corps Second Lieutenant Clebe McClary was an infantry officer in 1968. One afternoon, helicopters transported McClary's thirteen-man patrol out to a tea plantation. The marines cleared away punji stake traps and mines, and camped for the night atop a hill near the tea plantation. At midnight, NVA troops armed with hand grenades and **satchel charges** attacked McClary's marines. "They had grenades around their waists [with] the pins pulled, killing themselves, trying to kill us," he remembers. An NVA soldier charged, and McClary shot him. As he fell, the NVA soldier's satchel charge exploded. "I … the blast had blown my left arm off just above the elbow," McClary said.

Every soldier had a flak jacket, a kind of armored vest that protected him against sharp pieces of metal, called shrapnel, that buzzed through the air after a mine or **mortar** bomb exploded. Sometimes soldiers brought heavier armor to protect them on patrol. For example, one U.S. officer described how his infantry used tracked armored vehicles, and how the terrain sometimes made it difficult to use them: "We did not pursue the enemy in [the M113 Armored Personnel Carrier (APC)]," Smith said. "We used the tracks as a means of transportation. We used the tracks for protection from sniper fire while bringing in artillery and air strikes. And we used the tracks for the firepower of their .50-caliber machine guns."

Most patrols involved light infantry mounted aboard helicopters. If a lightly armed squad got hit while on patrol, the soldiers could radio back for heavier firepower. But the Viet Cong learned to hold fire until the patrol was at its most vulnerable and the helicopters had left. They chose their targets carefully too. Specialist Richard J. Hayes, an assistant squad leader with Second Platoon, C Company, First **Battalion**, Tenty-seventh Infantry recalls:

"We landed ... in an open field about ten meters or fifteen meters from [an embankment]. As the last bird lifted off the ground, then ... [the Viet Cong] opened up with AK47 [automatic rifles] and rocket-propelled grenades. We heard people screaming for the medic, but there was nothing the medic could do. He was dead. The medic got shot right away."

FRAGGING

Sometimes, discipline in U.S. fighting units broke down completely. Some soldiers mutinied or deserted their posts. Others lashed out at their superiors. "Fragging" referred to the attempted murder or actual murder of an officer, characteristically with a fragmenting hand grenade. According to the Office of the Secretary of the Navy, between 1964 and 1972, 122 marines were charged with murder or attempted murder. Army units reported a total of 1,016 fragging incidents.

Left: Artillery units were critical to the success of infantry operations. For troops ambushed by the Viet Cong while on patrol, air strikes might arrive too late. Infantrymen depended upon the artillery to provide immediate fire support.

Daily Life

Right: Marines such as these, pictured eating C rations, adapted to the rugged conditions of daily life in the field. Men looked forward to moving back to larger base camps, however, where the amenities were more like those at home.

Daily life south of the Demilitarized Zone (DMZ) had many hardships and few comforts. The DMZ was the dividing line between North and South Vietnam established by a conference in Geneva, Switzerland, in 1954. The DMZ cut west to east at the seventeenth parallel.

LIFE IN THE FIELD

Out in the field, soldiers spent a lot of their free time cleaning their equipment and weapons to be ready for the next patrol. As troops learned lessons fighting in Southeast Asia, the government improved their equipment. New tropical combat uniforms were made of tougher and cooler fabric. The soldiers' boots were made tougher, too, to resist punji stakes. On patrol, marines and soldiers learned to carry more water, ammunition, and hand grenades in place of extra food and clothing. In the field, soldiers often ate C rations: boxed meals with canned main courses, such as beans and meat; cans of fruit; a dessert, such as a sweet cake; chewing gum; and other small luxuries. South Vietnamese soldiers ate more traditional foods. One U.S. Army adviser said he spent mealtimes with a Vietnamese comrade, eating "exactly what [the Vietnamese] was eating, which was sufficient and in certain cases was more than I could eat." A typical Vietnamese meal included rice, which each soldier boiled in his own small pot, and vegetables.

With help from letters and packages sent from home, many soldiers overcame the hardships of the field and found ways to make their daily lives more bearable, according to Second Lieutenant Tim Lickness of the 101st Airborne Brigade.

"We became accomplished cooks, combining C rations with sauces sent from home. We sealed envelopes, whose glue became useless from the humidity, with peach jam. We heated meals with fuel made from peanut butter and insect repellent. We buoyed our

29

Above: In the field, men found some time to relax amid the terrors of combat. Here, a marine reads from a paperback Western novel while having a snack. Note the captured Vietnamese field glasses around his neck.

morale by describing our favorite meal, favorite car, or favorite girl back home. We lived for letters and care packages from the U.S."

LIFE IN BASE CAMPS

When they stood-down after months in the field, soldiers would go to larger installations, called base camps. ("Standing down" refers to a period of rest and refitting in which all operational activity, except for security, is stopped.) These installations provided hot showers and beds and a small Post Exchange store, also called a PX, where soldiers could buy junk food—such as soda and candy—magazines, toiletries, and other things they required or that simply reminded them of home. Base camps also had enlisted men's clubs, where the grunts could buy beer and watch movies. Soldiers also held cookouts and played games like baseball and volleyball to keep up morale.

Soldiers lived in "hooch" barracks, buildings that housed several men and their possessions. South Vietnamese civilian women, called "Mama Sans" by the soldiers, worked at the hooch. The Mama Sans were paid servants who cleaned the hooch and did the troops' laundry. Often, lines hung with drying laundry were stretched across the alleys between hooch buildings.

Base camp also provided the venue for government-sponsored live shows, which also helped raise troops' morale. The United Service Organizations (USO) had organized musical variety stage shows since World War II. The shows often brought celebrities, such as comedian Bob Hope, and famous singers and actors to perform for the soldiers. Former Marine Corps Commandant General James L. Jones said he remembered his men looking forward to USO shows even when they did not have permission to go to see them.

"One afternoon, my radio operator and a couple other Marines were going to make a PX run on behalf of the platoon to buy towels, soap, and toothpaste. Knowing that they were going to where the USO show was being held, I admonished them that they were to return as soon as possible because we were going to go on patrol that night. Night came and went without a sign of them. When they sheepishly rolled up in the morning, they explained that the opportunity to see the show was just too good to pass up. They dug fighting holes for the rest of the platoon for a month."

Left: Few things boosted morale better than hot food from back home, even under less-than-ideal conditions. Here, marines at Khe Sanh pause for a meal of canned stew, which they have heated on portable stoves.

THE COUNTERCULTURE

Above: Actress Jane Fonda was an outspoken critic of the war and caused controversy by being photographed visiting an NVA air defense artillery site near Hanoi in 1971. She later apologized for her actions.

From the mid-1960s through the end of U.S. combat troops' involvement in Vietnam in 1973, young people in the United States and elsewhere energized a new era of artistic, musical, social, and political expression known as the counterculture movement. It was characterized by self-expression and an emphasis on a peaceful and loving approach to art and to life.

The movement was a forum for social activism, promoting social equality and individual freedom. Young people questioned traditional values and demanded civil rights for ethnic minorities and equal rights for women.

For the soldiers fighting in Vietnam, the counterculture movement back home in the United States raised troubling issues. Some soldiers began to question the morality of the war and to rebel against strict military discipline, although most soldiers served their tours of duty honorably.

With war and social unrest tearing at the heart of American culture, many U.S. troops found the public either indifferent or hostile to them and to their experiences. Some critics of the war blamed all soldiers for the high-profile crimes of a few, such as the massacre at My Lai.

THE WIDER PICTURE

By the late 1960s, soldiers fighting in Vietnam knew that many people in the United States were against the war. Activist groups, such as the Entertainment Industry for Peace and Justice, worked to voice many people's resentments toward the military. Celebrities, such as actress Jane Fonda, organized antimilitary and antiwar demonstrations outside U.S. bases. The antiwar movement in the United States and elsewhere in the world undermined support for the conflict, both at home and on the front lines.

In 1971, Fonda made a high-profile tour of North Vietnam. She visited NVA officials at Hanoi, posed for a photograph beside communist soldiers at an anti-aircraft gun emplacement, and denounced U.S. policy. Many war veterans described Fonda's visit to North Vietnam as a betrayal of her country and accused her of collaborating with the enemy.

While many soldiers were deeply committed to fighting communism, others began to question whether the United States should be involved in Vietnam. Some soldiers applied for status as "conscientious objectors," to be excused from fighting on religious

U.S.–VIETNAMESE RELATIONS

Many of the soldiers saw Vietnam as part of "the inscrutable Orient," an alien world. According to Marine Corps Major Kenneth E. Wynn, sometimes soldiers had racist attitudes. "Throughout a Marine's military development, the Vietnamese people, North and South, were saddled with negative connotations," Wynn said. Many others respected their South Vietnamese allies, however. Army Captain Joseph W. Kinzer, who served with U.S. Advisory Team 163, explained:

"[A soldier] had to realize his situation. [The Vietnamese] had been at war a long time and did not have a lot to look forward to. An American spent a year in Vietnam or two years and then went home to the States. ... For the Vietnamese, it was more of the same, day after day."

Right: The war continued despite holidays such as Christmas, and soldiers longed for news of home. Here at a Special Forces camp, men read their mail amid small Christmas trees decorating their otherwise drab green tents.

or moral grounds. Even the U.S. Armed Forces Radio and Television Service, which broadcast news and entertainment programs to the troops in the field, played antiwar songs.

Soldiers in Vietnam were also affected by the movement back in the United States demanding civil rights for African Americans and other minorities. Although the process of desegregation had begun during the Korean War (1950–1953), the Vietnam War was the first conflict in which an entirely desegregated military fought. Discrimination continued, however, with minorities usually holding lower-level jobs compared to their white counterparts. That balance began to shift during the Vietnam War. African Americans led combat patrols, piloted close air-support missions, and served in senior staff positions at headquarters. Among ground troops, more than 41,000 African American marines served. Five African American marines earned the Congressional Medal of Honor in Vietnam.

Sometimes the same tensions that led to riots and other violence back home in the United States erupted into conflicts

FIREBASES

A firebase was a temporary fortification built to house mobile field artillery and infantry. Firebases usually had embankments for six-gun batteries of 4.1-inch (105-mm) and 6.1-inch (155-mm) howitzers or bigger guns. The guns were arranged in star-shaped patterns of five howitzers, with a sixth in the center. The artillery was positioned in a variety of places, or could be moved quickly, to counter attacks and to support U.S. and allied infantry. Soldiers defended a perimeter around their firebases with sandbagged machine gun bunkers, rifle pits, trenches, and concertina razor wire guarding the big guns. Firebases also had landing pads for helicopters to carry infantry out into the bush on patrol.

Above: At firebases, artillery crews manned guns that provided fire support to infantry patrols operating nearby. Here, a gun crew adjusts the fire of its 4.1-inch (105-mm) howitzer in response to a call radioed from the field.

among soldiers. For the most part, however, the shared trauma of the war tended to bring soldiers closer together, regardless of their ethnicity. Many black veterans remember their service in Vietnam as having afforded them more equality of treatment than they received from civilian society when they returned home.

Women also took part in the drama of daily life in Vietnam. Although exact figures are hard to come by, it is estimated that between 7,500 and 11,000 women served in various branches of the military in Vietnam, the majority as nurses.

CHAPTER 4: Rest and Relaxation

On Leave

Right: At R&R facilities, soldiers could relax and almost forget about the war for a while. One might never realize from this photograph that a guerrilla war raged in the jungle a few tens of miles away from these men tanning on the beach at the resort of Vung Tau.

Every soldier could take a week of leave during his tour of duty. Many chose to spend their leave at a rest and recreation (R&R) center in-country. One of the most famous was the China Beach R&R Center at Da Nang. China Beach was a coastal resort where soldiers could lie on the beach, go swimming, work out at a gymnasium, or play softball and other sports. The center had a large PX and cafeteria as well.

CITY TEMPTATIONS

Other troops chose to spend leave outside Vietnam. Soldiers visited Hong Kong, Taiwan, Thailand, Japan, and Australia. Their commanders, however, warned them to be careful when they were abroad. Russian and Chinese spies tried to glean information from the U.S. personnel that could be useful to the NVA and the Viet Cong. For example, one soldier related the following: "I went to Japan on R&R for a week. On the street, I was approached by a Russian agent trying to get information about our unit in Vietnam."

Often soldiers visited Saigon, a bustling metropolis in South Vietnam. Large markets there sold everything: food, souvenirs, cameras and electronics, music, and western liquor and tobacco. Soldiers rented motorcycles or hired pedicabs and cyclos— motorized bicycle taxis—to take them shopping around the city. A black market also thrived in Saigon, offering counterfeit watches and jewelry, stolen goods, and narcotics. Downtown, soldiers could visit movie theaters, restaurants, nightclubs, and massage parlors. Beneath the chaotic capitalism of Saigon, danger lurked. Viet Cong agents moved freely throughout the city, secretly working against the government of South Vietnam. Some of these guerrillas carried out terrorist bombings and sniper attacks in the city.

Navy Lieutenant Commander Bobbi Hovis of the Nurse Corps said, "Life never returned to normal while I was in

Right: Some U.S. soldiers used drugs to escape the grimness of their experiences in the war; others simply took advantage of the easy availability of drugs on the black market of Southeast Asia.

DRUGS

Some soldiers used illegal drugs during their tours in Vietnam. Drugs such as marijuana, heroin, and raw opium were commonplace. Between 1969 and 1972, Marine Corps records show that 5,136 marines were discharged from service because of drug offenses. During the same time period, more than 4,210 other marines were charged but not thrown out of the service. According to another Marine Corps report, 48 percent of Marine troops in Vietnam said they had used drugs. As the war ground on, drug use increased, according to Department of Defense records. In 1970, the army reported 17,742 investigations of drug offenses. From 1968 to 1972, the total number of verified cases of addiction throughout the armed forces nearly doubled.

Vietnam. There was always an undercurrent of unrest from one faction or another."

Eventually, as U.S. commanders tried to increase security and curb soldiers' use of drugs and prostitutes, soldiers had to follow strict curfews and restrictions on the places they could visit while in Saigon and other cities.

PROSTITUTION

Prostitution was a major industry throughout Southeast Asia, not just in Saigon and other Vietnamese cities. Soldiers visited so-called "massage parlors" offering steam baths and more intimate services. Walking the streets and in the night clubs of Bangkok, Hong Kong, Taipei, and Manila were large numbers of prostitutes hoping to profit from the soldiers. A consequence of the large market for prostitutes was the spread of venereal diseases, which reached epidemic proportions among some U.S. units and prompted commanders to close down brothels and impose curfews.

Left: Small brothels, such as this one in Saigon, catered to the American servicemen and their U.S. dollars, which went very far in the depressed economy of wartime Vietnam.

Going Home

Right: For many wounded soldiers, a MEDEVAC flight was the first step in the long road to recovery and returning back home. Here, a U.S. Marine signals a UH-1 Huey to take off from a wooded clearing near Da Nang in 1967.

According to the U.S. Veterans' Administration, 9.2 million Americans served in the military between 1964 and 1975. There were 3.1 million service men and women deployed to Southeast Asia. Of that total, 47,410 were killed in combat. There were 10,788 non-combat-related deaths in Southeast Asia. There were 153,303 Americans wounded during the war.

All soldiers looked forward to their Expiration of Term of Service (ETS), when their thirteen-month tour of duty ended, and they would go back home to the United States. A soldier whose tour of duty was coming to an end was called a "short timer." When the time came to go home, soldiers would report to a base and turn in their field equipment. They were assigned a place on one of the fourteen-hour flights to the United States, often on board an air force C-141 Starlifter transport or sometimes a civilian airliner.

Most soldiers returning home from Vietnam were able to resume a normal life in civilian society. Many veterans left military service and took up jobs as laborers and businessmen, teachers, doctors, lawyers, and politicians. Others chose to take advantage of the experience and training they had received and continued their career in the military after the war.

However, many veterans were terribly affected by their experiences in Vietnam. Some veterans reported facing conflict at home, between the traumatic experiences of war and the tenor of civilian life. Some civilians who objected to the Vietnam War also expressed hostility toward the troops who fought.

"I went [to Vietnam] waving the flag; I went there very patriotic, wanting to really do a good job as a soldier," army

THE UH-1 IROQUOIS

The Huey, as it was nicknamed, came to be the most common utility helicopter in Vietnam. The Army, Air Force, Marine Corps, and Navy used these choppers as transports and gun ships and for "dust-offs"—medical evacuations, named after the dust thrown up by the rotor blades.

Right: Soldiers
looked forward to
the end of their
tours of duty. With
the date of their
return flights home
approaching, the
men's spirits lifted.

chaplain Captain Al Arvay said. "When I came home … I had
some very strange experiences. I had people who would get
very angry just … seeing the uniform. It was very difficult."

Soldiers who were wounded in action often returned home
before their tours of duty ended. Military medics often were the
first to treat combat casualties and prepare them for emergency
evacuation. "War is … just organized hell," said Al Rascon, an
army medic who won the Congressional Medal of Honor.
"During the time I was in Vietnam, 1965 to 1966, I took care
of people who were critically injured. I took care of people who
died in my arms."

Army medics, and navy hospital corpsmen who served with
the marines, often risked their lives in combat to treat wounded
soldiers. Like other soldiers, a medic was trained in basic combat
skills, but he often went unarmed into danger. Medics flew into
the combat zone on UH–1 Huey helicopters specially marked
with a white square and red cross. These choppers were
dedicated to carrying wounded **GIs** back to an aid station
or hospital, depending on the severity of their injuries.

HOSPITAL CORPSMEN

Navy medics, known as hospital corpsmen, have served with Marine Corps combat units since 1798. The Marine Corps has long had a close traditional relationship with the navy, traveling aboard navy ships and working alongside sailors. Hospital corpsmen were trained at Field Medical Service Schools at Marine Corps Base Camp Pendleton, California, and at Marine Corps Base Camp Lejeune, North Carolina. The schools taught corpsmen how to save lives on a battlefield under fire. The job was dangerous and stressful. Many of the Marine Corps' casualties in Vietnam were life-threatening trauma injuries from gunshots or shrapnel. The corpsman had to patch up casualties amid combat before the dust-offs arrived.

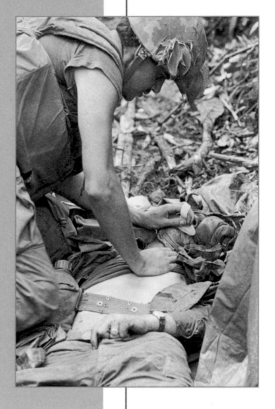

Above: Unarmed medics helped save wounded men's lives, often at the risk of their own.

For soldiers who were badly injured, the journey home was the beginning of a tough adjustment. Many who were wounded in action had to face the hardship of life from a wheelchair or with other handicaps. There are, however, inspiring stories of men and women who were able to overcome their disabilities and go on to live full lives, often helping other veterans.

For example, David Gorman lost both legs in Vietnam. He went on to become the executive director of Disabled American Veterans. This organization was formed in 1920 and chartered by the Congress in 1932 to help wounded veterans regain their health and succeed in civilian society.

Time Line

1955: October, South Vietnam officially becomes the Republic of Vietnam (RVN).

1962: Military Assistance Command, Vietnam (MACV) is established in Saigon.

1964: August, USS *Maddox* is reportedly attacked by North Vietnamese in Gulf of Tonkin; Congress passes the Gulf of Tonkin Resolution.

1965: October, 6,000 NVA and Viet Cong troops attack a U.S. Special Forces Base in the Ia Drang Valley. The U.S. Army's 1st Cavalry Division enters a monthlong battle.

1966: January, U.S. and South Vietnamese troops attack Viet Cong bases in the "Iron Triangle," a Viet Cong-dominated area north of Saigon.

1968: January, Tet Offensive is launched against Saigon, Hue, and other cities, and Marine Corps bases including Khe Sanh.

1969: January, President Richard M. Nixon announces a policy to strengthen the role of the Army of the Republic of Vietnam under a program called "Vietnamization."

1970: Widespread demonstrations against the war in the U.S.; December, Congress repeals the Gulf of Tonkin Resolution.

1972: December, Operation Linebacker begins.

1973: January, peace accords are signed in Paris, France; March, last U.S. ground troops leave Vietnam.

1975: January, North Vietnam announces an all-out offensive to seize South Vietnam; April, last U.S. citizens are evacuated from Saigon; North Vietnamese take Saigon the next day.

Glossary

artillery: large-barreled, crew-served mounted weapons

battalion: military unit composed of three or more companies

cavalry: combat troops mounted in vehicles, armored vehicles, and/or helicopters

court-martial: a judicial court for trying members of the armed services

GIs: a member of the U.S. armed forces

guerrilla: a person who engages in irregular warfare, especially as a member of an independent unit carrying out harassment or acts of sabotage

indoctrination: instruction in fundamental ideas in order to imbue with a particular point of view

infantry: soldiers trained to fight on foot

mortar: a short, large-caliber cannon that fires high into the air

parole: the release of a prisoner before the expiration of his or her other sentence on the promise of good behavior

platoon: a military unit composed of two or more squads

reveille: a bugle call at about sunrise signaling the first military formation of the day

satchel charge: small bag packed with explosives, usually detonated by means of a fuse

squad: the smallest military tactical unit

Further Reading

BOOKS

Adler, Bill (Editor). *Letters from Vietnam.* New York: Presidio Press/Ballantine Books, 2003.

Cash, John A., et al. *Seven Firefights in Vietnam.* Washingtion D.C.: U.S. Army Office of the Chief of Military History/U.S. Government Printing Office, 1985.

Chatfield, Charles. *The American Peace Movement: Ideals and Activism.* New York: Twayne, 1992.

Hess, Martha. *Then the Americans Came: Voices from Vietnam.* New York: Four Walls Eight Windows, 1993.

Terry, Wallace. *Bloods: An Oral History of the Vietnam War by Black Veterans.* New York: Random House, 1984.

WEB SITES

The Public Broadcasting System: American Experience
www.pbs.org/wgbh/amex/vietnam/
An online program with a time line of the Vietnam War.

The U.S. Army Center for Military History
www.army.mil/cmh/online/Bookshelves/VN.htm
An online database of information on the Vietnam War and other conflicts.

The Virtual Vietnam Archive of the Vietnam Project, Texas Tech University
www.vietnam.ttu.edu/
A large database of Vietnam War documents online.

The Vietnam Database
www.thevietnam-database.co.uk/
A site, according to its creators, that is "an almanac for Vietnam re-enactors, collectors, and living history groups."

Index